A SPAR

by

Apawaae

Labyrinth Books

First edition published by

Labyrinth Books
Vestry Hall
High Street
Glastonbury BA6 9DU

Telephone 01458 830831

labyrinthbooks@aol.com

Cover design and photography
Chris Render

Technical assistance
Abby Render

isbn 978-0-9558737-0-6

Printed in England by Booksprint

CONTENTS

1	The Opening	5
2	Clear Sight	6
3	Sacred Places	10
4	Darkness	14
5	What is a Magic Symbol?	18
6	Time	24
7	The Eight Festivals – A Magical Perspective	28
8	The Legend of a Witch Name	32
9	Levels of Being	36
10	Initiation	41
11	The Magic Loop	45
12	The Chalice	49
13	More than a Word	53
14	The Crown	57
15	The Importance of Preparation	61
16	A Universal symbol	65
17	The Book of Books	69
18	The Word Least Understood	73
19	A Spark of Wonder	77
20	The Closing	81

"THE WRITER"

THE OPENING

At the outset, the reader is justified in asking, "Why write and publish words on magic, especially given that, contained within these writings, is a section outlining the difficulties and folly of trying to learn from books. So, given this strongly held view, why add another publication to the pile?"

In defence it must be stated that this is not a book of instruction, far from it. It is a series of words written about esoteric magic and written in the way of esoteric magic. As such, it is appropriate for those who are either seeking a way that is right for them or for those who have already found a way. The words apply just as well to both.

Most instruction in esoteric magic is carried out within the respective organisations and this is how it should be, for the teachings are for the few. Indeed it must be emphasised that the inner way is for the few.

The concept that the good word must be spread far and wide so that as many people as possible can participate is evangelical and exoteric. Whilst the motive may be pure, the results are most definitely not.

We will let what follows speak for itself and, if a glimmer of hope is ignited in just one soul who feels lost in the quest, then it will have been a worthwhile endeavour.

CLEAR SIGHT

Clairvoyance means clear sight. Clear sight means seeing things as they really are. Not how we would like them to be; not how we fear that they might be, or could be, or should be. With clairvoyance there is no ambiguity. Clear sight is clear sight.

The practitioner of esoteric magic knows, however, that reality is mostly beyond the limitations of the human brain. Therefore a simplistic approach to seeing reality will always be inadequate. The world of the true clairvoyant is a world of analogy, for it is only by analogy that reality can be identified. As a result, each practitioner will see in a different way. For example, the vision of the inner worlds experienced by Emanuel Swedenborg is vastly different from that experienced by the Siberian shaman, yet both are true.

Before continuing, it would be right to mention that this paper is not about fortune telling, or more accurately, predicting the future. Certainly clear sight is used for this purpose, but it is only one small aspect of its use. It is also an opportunity to point out that the future is not fixed. Clairvoyance will show the likely outcome in the existing set of circumstances, but we all have the right to deal with that set of circumstances if it is within our powers and ability. Karma is very much about dealing with those things put before us; it is not about blindly accepting our fate.

Let us start by looking upon clear sight from a different perspective; from the perspective of those who are naturally sensitive to the world of esoteric magic. For these people clear sight begins with an inner knowing. There is that within that tells them that there is something more; something that cannot be found in the manifest world alone. At some point all of these people will take tentative steps towards finding out about this pull to the centre, this inner knowing that cannot be explained. Most will only ever make that initial tentative response. Others will, sadly, get lost along the way for false paths are legion. They will do this for many reasons. It may be fear of the need to struggle for illumination, fear of responsibility, ego, genuine illusion, falling for the promises of bogus spiritual guides, the need for community (It can be a lonely journey), and so on.

The observation that many are called but few are chosen is all too real in the esoteric world and, true to this phrase, there will be a final few who will spend there lives making the effort to see their vision through; to play their part in bringing through the light in whichever way they have chosen. They know that their journey began with this inner knowing (their first clear sight) and the rest of their work will always involve seeking a clearer view of the reality behind all; the evolutionary reality known only to the mystic and esoteric practitioner of magic; for clear sight provides signposts that give direction, direction to the source of that inner knowing.

From me all things proceed and into me all things must return.

For in this life, the ones who have chosen to walk the path will say,

> "I am of the earth and in the earth,
> A beacon in my hand.
> I am of the earth and in the earth,
> Here I make my stand."

In this respect, clear sight is a tool to help in the chosen work. To use this valuable tool, techniques must be developed. There are many. Some will try a prayer to their Deity saying, "Show me". Rarely are such prayers answered, at least, not to the expectation of the one who is asking.

Practitioners of magic use a wide range of tools and techniques and, used properly, they all work. There are crystals, pendulums, tarot card, I Ching, runes, magic mirrors, numerology, scrying in the spirit vision, meditation techniques, dreams, holy writings, etc. There is also clear sight that will come spontaneously at any time, day or night.

To the practitioner of magic, a controlled system is preferable. It keeps the work focussed in a properly prepared way and is usually done in a properly prepared place. This avoids the confusion that surrounds many natural psychics. Properly constructed rituals are also an excellent way of keeping to the right path for those who are able to use them.

As stated earlier, karma is our earthly test. No one is excluded. The laws of karma apply just as much to the magician as they do to any other person. Magicians, like anybody else, choose their path in this life and, at its end, they too will enter the same judgement halls. By their deeds shall they be known. The ways of achievement may differ but the karmic law is the same. They too are faced with difficulties. They too are faced with limitations and boundaries against which they must earn the right to push back or move beyond.

By trial and error clear sight is developed and successful clear sight is usually accompanied with a feeling of knowing that it is right. There simply is no doubt. These are the good times.

If it were that easy, however, the world would be choked with successful visionaries. In reality there are so many things that can cloud the outcome. Emotional involvement is notorious for blocking clairvoyance. Looking for the answer that we want is another common problem. The mind must be totally open to good and bad or light and dark at all times if there is to be an honest assessment. Personal agendas will also close the door as will the easy trap of becoming a message junky who needs council for every move; clear sight cannot take away personal responsibility. There will also be times when we are simply not meant to see and it is important to recognise these times and to look no further.

> Be cleansed in beauty.
> Be cleansed by fire.
> Be cleansed by mercy.
> Call into the dark, the vast, the endless space.
> See sorrow, know hollow, be truly alone.
> Die in that place again and again,
> But not in illusion.
> Know, not assume.
> Know, not pretend.
> Go there and know
> The ultimate end that can never end.
> She will be waiting.
> Unknown, Unknowable,
> All.

When a technique has been found that works, the following pointers are well worth bearing in mind. Scryers nearly always see in symbols and the real skill is not so much in seeing the images, but in interpreting the meaning of the symbols. As stated earlier, analogy is the way of the clairvoyant. There will also be times when no clear sight will come. Accept these times for no amount of forcing will change things. Also never censor your vision, no matter how erroneous it may seem.

A true test is knowing when it is appropriate to use clairvoyance and when it is not. Only experience will help in this respect. Never expect easy answers, for remember, some of the greatest visions of the ancient past are still being interpreted and interpreted on many levels. The most famous in the western world is probably the vision of Ezekiel.

You may one day be blessed with your own great vision, your guiding light; something that influences your own chosen work. If so, to thine own self be true whilst always keeping pure your highest ideal; for then your light will not become an end in itself but a glorious tool in the service of your Deity.

3

SACRED PLACES

Not so long ago, these words were taken down during a visit to Glastonbury.

THE TROUBLES OF THE TOR   *by Apawaae*

I suck, I thirst, I need sustain
I cry, I lie, I dream, I aim.
I do and do and do until
I cannot find the driving will.

I must fulfil, I must retain
The will to live and know again
The needs of those who bring their pain
To me.

My way was given by those of old
To take the needing unto my fold.
To hold them there and give them life.
To show them love and share their strife.

I had the way, I had the will.
I knew how they could feed and fill
Themselves from my free gift of life,
But now all's left is toil and strife.

I must fulfil, it is my charge.
I'll do those things that can be done.
I'll suck, I'll lie, I'll do all things
To bless the askers and set them free.

But I am weary,
I am spent.
I need to feel a few repent.
I need a gift, a knowing one.

I need to feel the olden ones
Who gave me life
To deal with strife
And light the light
Of those who call.

May the candle ever burn.
May the olden ones return
And feed my fire
And drive my soul
And I will live
And make all whole
Who truly seek the way

And live the trusting way

And give to all as I

And need no more to lie

Or suck or see them die

From my spent soul.

These words will resonate with those versed in esoteric magic and know that sacred places don't just happen to be there; they are not geographic accidents. Far from it, they are made. There are many sacred places upon this earth. Places where the veil is thin and in England Glastonbury Tor is one of the best known and most visited.

In all schools of western magic (and mysticism) where practitioners work with the forces beyond manifestation, they must first create a place between the worlds, a place of communion. It can be a physically drawn circle or a visualised circle that is ritually cleansed. For the most able (and they are as rare as snow in august) it can be within the self. It can be a temple built of stone where genuine acts of devotion take place at regular intervals. It can be a sacred grove, or a cave, or a cathedral. What is universal to all of these is the need to make the place pure and free from the influence of malignant forces, however they are perceived. Also universal is the need to "influence" the spiritual powers in these places for the perceived good in whatever way it is defined by the practitioners, be they pagans, Christians or of any other path.

There is a law, a law of duality. Therefore only by giving can one receive and the priesthood of temples give in many ways. It may be devotion, or personal sacrifice, hard labour for their cause, or the raising of pure and focussed energy. Giving to the highest in order to bring through a blessing to the world.

It would be wrong to say that all so called practitioners of esoteric magic work in this way. Our world is as full of false prophets as it always has been. Illusion and escapism are very easy traps to fall into. Glastonbury, as much as any other place, has its share of these traps and each must decide for themselves as to the worth of what is on offer.

Let us dwell no more upon this aspect and focus instead upon the future of sacred places and the Tor in particular. Many people visit the Tor. Most are tourists who enjoy its unique beauty and the challenging pleasure of climbing to the summit to admire the wonderful views. These people are, in the main, good souls who have little direct influence on the aspects with which we have a concern. Then there are the "spiritual tourists" who visit purely to soak up whatever is there. These are of concern. There are also those people who have a genuine need, who visit the Tor with a cry for help. They have every right to do so, for it is a place where the veil is thin and a call will be heard; but for how long? And how many return to give thanks when their call is answered?

Let us return to those enigmatic, poetic words above. Let us contemplate the law of duality. Let us think back to those ancient days when generations of people created a holy place at Glastonbury, specifically the Tor. For how much longer can people draw upon the blessing created when the link was made between the earth and the high spiritual realms? Where are the priestesses and priests who give to the highest so that the window can remain open? It is reciprocation that takes the great work forward, and even then, the most successful works are but tiny glittering drops in an ocean that is vaster than we can ever know.

Sacred places are created and the window will only remain open for as long as those who are able continue to give. We humbly ask that, next time you visit a place that is sacred, treat it as you would treat your own temple and, in your own way, give a gift to the highest.

We will be the fire that heats the cauldron. Most will come, drink all they see and move on. But some will sip and realise its infinite vastness and stay.

REFINING THE PENDULUM.

It is easy to get lost in the distracting clouds that are created around "spiritual places". They are halfway houses of illusion and the unscrupulous and misguided are very willing to use them. Another way of feeding off that which was given of old and also the vulnerable on their journey. Duality is reality. No one can leap from a sodden mire or grasp falling water as it cascades from above. Needless to say it is better to seek a firmer foundation than these and use the water to cleanse.

Fearing the dark or denying the night is a journey taken halfway. Wholeness is in the falling night and the dawning day. For some it is the aleph and the heh. For others mercy and severity. Clarity arises from conquering confusion. The hidden is not revealed by gazing into the dark alone. There is always a price to pay.

And for those who say, "Long and loud was my call, yet all that I heard was silence", the wise reply, "Then listen again in another way".

Mighty are the holy twin pillars, the pylon, the well-guarded gate.

4

DARKNESS

What did they see in the darkness that was so inspired?
What did they see in the darkness that was so desired?

Many will see the darkness as a place of fear; the sort of fear that they remember from their childhood days. It is a fear of the unknown. Others, more enlightened, will say that the darkness is necessary for, without it, we cannot know the light. They will be right, but if we choose to use this argument, we must also accept that we cannot know the darkness without knowing the light.

To those who take the simplistic view, light represents everything that is good and darkness represents everything else. As a form of symbolism, it works, but with significant limitations for, to apply this theory, a subjective and judgemental decision has to be made in order to define what is good and what is not. In other words, the observer tells the two symbols what they represent. This is an extremely limited process that offers little or nothing to the serious student of the occult. It is a truly exoteric approach well beloved of those who think that they have solved all mysteries and have God on their side.

Let us look at darkness from another perspective. Let us consider darkness to be the place where all that we do not know is hidden (for occult means hidden). Given that we can only learn those things that we do not know, this makes the darkness a much more meaningful thing. It also gives a more meaningful definition to the light, for the terms revelation and illumination then make better sense.

> I gaze into the dark
> And silence overwhelms.
> I gaze into the dark,
> To a myriad of realms.
> I see boats that ply these ways
> With Great Ones at the helms.

To a student of the occult, a flash of divine inspiration alone is only the beginning. The next part of the work rests in learning to understand, harness and use that vision; a genuine work of light. How students, or initiates, do this will vary greatly, but sound principles apply and they are universal to all systems.

We cannot look into the darkness without shining a light for groping in the dark is not seeing. However, no one can shine a light unless they have the means to do so. In the world of magic and mysticism the lantern that is used is nothing less than the ability of the operator. Like any other lantern it has to be carefully made and maintained so that it becomes a reliable and trusted tool. In time it can be refined to a greater level of efficiency or be replaced by an even better one as the skill of the operator improves.

All schools of magic and mysticism have their established techniques that have been tried and tested. All help to create the lantern. They include such skills as meditation and contemplation, the controlled use of dreams, ritual magic with its focussed blast of power, intense concentration, acts of devotion, use of symbolic keys and so on. They have been used either separately or in combination in one form or another for many centuries and will continue to be used until a better way is found; which will be, of course, another refinement of the lantern.

None of these techniques are easy. The practitioner is entering into the unknown and, as is universally accepted in all walks of life, nothing worthwhile ever comes easily.

There are dangers. They can be managed but they do exist and let none tell you otherwise. These dangers are of a minor nature for most people and are linked, in the main, to their level of ability. Those who are on the fringe, or dabble, rarely put themselves at risk. Theirs is usually nothing more than a case of waywardness brought on by wishful thinking and the temptation of searching for the outcome that they would prefer to see.

It will be found that the well-trained practitioner takes a great deal of time and trouble to avoid the dangers. The ones who are most likely to fall into the trap are those who have a little genuine ability and who become cocky and casual; also those who are naturally open but lack any real form of control, the ones who are often called natural psychics. For both of these the dangers span from being trapped in illusion in all its forms, leading up to emotional and mental instability. What they do is expose themselves to all of the astral influences (and effluent) that exist thereby picking up any old random impressions that come their way. Worse still, they may pick up "spirit guides" that are only too willing to latch on to them. In other words, they make a veritable trawl of the astral influences without any means of control or discrimination.

There are very good reasons why magic or "the mysteries" is a way for the few. A scalpel is a wonderful tool as long as it is held in the hand of a qualified surgeon.

Returning to our theme. We are considering the darkness as a place where all knowledge lies hidden. It is for a good reason that, on the Cabalistic Tree of Life, Daath lies in the abyss. It is also for a good reason that this "Sephirah that is not" does not appear on the Tree of Life when it is correctly depicted as a glyph.

> I gaze into a room
> Without windows or a door.
> I gaze into a room
> Without walls, a ceiling or floor.

For most of us, the best lantern that we can make is but a flickering candle that gutters in the eternal cosmic wind. Even so, each flicker of light, if created by the will of a genuine seeker will, bit by bit, show another stone step on the upward winding mountain path. A stone step, a solid step, a rock. For this step must be a firm foundation; a foundation from which the next move will be made, both upwards in a continuance of the quest, and downwards in order to use that which has been revealed. It will be used in the way that the student chooses for, whilst the light may provide an insight and guidance, it will never replace the free will of the seer.

Those eternally patient ones who guide will say, "Let the lamp flame flicker until you see the flame come true". They have another concept of the darkness, a concept beyond our knowing where it is possible to be in the dark and know only light. It is another kind of light that is beyond the darkness. It is a place where there is neither night nor day.

Is this the jewel at the heart of the crown?

When journeying into the darkness, do so without expectation, for expectation is an imposition and an imposition prevents clear sight. We can only learn those things that we do not already know.

> A glass of clearest crystal
> Confronts my eye.
> A chalice?
> Does it contain or does it reveal?
> Or both?

5

WHAT IS A MAGIC SYMBOL?

Our world is full of symbols. We see them every day. Some fine examples are road signs where just two adjoining lines can clearly indicate a road junction and a wavy line shows a bumpy stretch of road. Another example is the plan of an electric circuit where symbols represent switches, fuse boxes and sockets. There are also the flags of nations that conjure up in our minds all that we know about the countries they portray. These symbols work. They work in a practical way, but they are not magic symbols.

Here is a random list of the types of symbols commonly associated with magic. There are talismans and amulets. There are tools and weapons such as wands, swords, the cup, the pentacle, the censor, perfumes and scents and lanterns and candles. There are crystals, robes and jewellery. Magic alphabets, tarot cards, runes, written words, the magic circle and its strange words. There is the pyramid and the altar. There are astrological signs such as the sun signs and the planetary symbols. There are the symbols of the occult elements, trees of life, crucifixes and other crosses. There are numbers and alphabets. There are symbolic sounds such as words of power and mantras. We also have symbolic movements in ritual using procession and dance. There are colours, the caduceus, magical names, magic squares and Egyptian symbols such as the ankh and scarab. There are visualised symbols, which includes most of those listed plus the Hebrew letters, the magic circle, personifications and blazing pentagrams. There are more.

Even though we know that these symbols repeatedly occur in magical systems, none of them are of any use whatsoever until they have been made so by the practitioner.

Let us start with a crude definition of magic. "To contact, commune with and influence the forces behind manifestation". There are better and more accurate descriptions by such people as Dion Fortune, A Crowley and W E Butler, but this one will do very well for our purposes.

Symbols are the language of magic. Almost all clairvoyance is achieved using symbols; and this is amply demonstrated by the continued use of tarot packs, runes and the I Ching. Symbols are also the tools of magic. They have been used as such for thousands of years, and the reason that they have been used is, quite simply, because they work. But before they can work, they have to be created.

Practitioners of magic know that there is a force behind manifestation. They also know that these forces can be influenced if the right methods are used. This brief explanation is not the place to debate or discuss the systems that exist, or the long training and practice that is required to master such skills. We are here concentrating on an explanation of the reason why symbols are used. It is necessary to state, however, that true and wise practitioners of esoteric magic work under the highest authority, the authority of Deity. How that Deity is understood is up to each individual, but "The One from Whom all things proceed and into Whom all things must return" is an essential part of their work. Each must be able to say, "May my will be Thy will". They also know of the absolute necessity of being properly prepared and of working in a properly prepared place. Anything less is dabbling.

Returning to our subject. Magic tools are symbols, but they have to be made to live, to become living symbols before they can be used in magic. Let us take as an example a wand. There are many types of wand. They can be made to represent spiritual fire, or procreative force, or the element air and so on. They can be as simple as a sapling cut from a tree or as complex as those wonderful examples of the "Golden Dawn" with their diverse colours and emblems such as crowns, hexagrams, lotus flowers, serpents and wings and the elements; symbols within symbols.

The process of ensouling the wand is as follows. Make it if at all possible. The more work a person puts into its construction, the better. If it does have to be acquired, then get a very basic wand so that the designs and colours can be added by the owner. No one can buy magic. No matter how expensive, no matter how beautiful, no matter how many words of recommendation come with a sword, or a talisman, or a ring, or anything else, it will not be a magical tool. The operator makes a magical weapon, not the vendor. Next, ensoul your wand with your will. Put everything you have into it. Consecrate it in whichever way is right for your system using water, incense, flame, oil, or whatever is right. Dedicate the wand to the work that it is made for and to the service of the highest. Make it holy. Finally, you must know that it will work. Know, not hope. Absolutely know. Only when you know that it will work will it be a true magical tool. From this point on take great care of the wand. Let no one else touch it. Never use it for any other purpose. Never let it come into contact with anything that can taint it and use it only at the appropriate time and in the appropriate place.

We use symbols to enable us, in a controlled way, to go beyond the rational, reductionist censor and work with the forces behind manifestation. We also use them as a language to commune with those forces. As already stated, there are many types of symbols.

Words, for example, are wonderful symbols when used magically. Magical words can be mantras, barbarous names, written emblems or enigmatic language. The use of enigmatic and often poetic words is important in ritual. If used correctly, the outer rational meaning fades and the inner unspoken is allowed to work. This is why rationalists can never explain magical language; they simply cannot understand its nature. Here are some enigmatic words. It is called "Saturn".

SATURN

"Experience is light", my dark lord said. Out of the night the blind will be led. Out of the dust the dry will be fed with waters that quench but never sate. "Experience is light", my dark lord said, "the waters you drink are earned ere they're fed. The waters you drink uplift the eye. To find a north way to cold and night sky". Frost, harsh, grips the wheel that plies this frozen way. Another step. Another day. The waters are cold; they melt in my head, loosening. "Experience is light", my dark lord said to me and green turf filled my eyes, free of the grip of winter. Softness of softness brushes the green about my feet. I step on water and air and frost again. "Experience is light", my dark lord said to me. "What melts the frost? What sets you free?

"Fire my lord, the fire within me. My fire fires the fire that lives eternally"

"Experience is light", my dark lord said to me.

I hope that you have found this book to be helpful and to finish here are some words about the making and use of a magic symbol. It is called "The Eye".

THE EYE

There was once a wise and noble one
Learned in arts arcane.
Long in the land was this noble one,
Keeping alight the flame.

She knew of Saturn's unbending law.
This land would soon be gone.
By hidden sea to another shore
Must journey this sagely one.

From child to maid she'd lived and played
As others of her age,
But a burning star, a fiery blade
Within began to rage.

Her quest began, her search was long
With many a fruitless day,
But as is written for the true and strong,
Someone will point the way.

Patience. Trust.

Long were the years and hard were the years
Reaping the seeds and sowing.
Facing the dark, facing all fears,
Edging towards the knowing.

She gave as they had given to her,
The ones who went before.
She guided the new along the way,
Each to their own chosen door.

But now the call is heard from on high;
In the ancient boat she'll ride.
Across the hidden sea she'll ply
Alone to the other side.

One last work on manifest earth
Was burning in her soul.
One last work, one final search
For the truth to make the whole.

An eye she sought, an eye all seeing,
The eye of ancient days.
An eye to show the final freeing
And bless these earthly ways.

Once only in this magicians time
Is a work allowed from so high.
Only in wisdoms elevated prime,
'Tis barred from others who try.

The time had come for the eye all seeing
To show her the open door,
But she must strive with all her being,
For none can change this law.

In the way of magic she chose to make
A symbol for her mission.
An eye created for her works sake.
An eye to see her vision.

She made the eye of matter and spirit,
No detail would she shirk.
She made the eye of matter and spirit.
No less would aid her work.

Then came the consecrations.
Then came the dedications.
To Goddess and God.
To the Infinite One.

Then came the application.

The eye was a key to the eye all seeing.
The way not easy or new,
But the life giving force of her very being
Opened the eye that was true.

And in the boat, rudder held steady
She carries a glorious light.
Daath. A knowing for the one who was ready
And a gift for us in the night.

She saw before her the all seeing eye
As did the wise of old.
She saw before her the eye of truth,
Penetrating and cold.

6

TIME

Time is a measure. It could be said that, in the way of the mysteries, time is *the* measure.

Before considering the nature of time, let us first use the power of our imagination to dwell upon the origin of all things. In Cabala it is called Ain. Of course the origin of all things cannot be known in terms that we understand for nothing was all and all was not. People have tried to come up with words to explain this state, words such as negativity, unbeing, non-existence and so on. In spite of these efforts, all are inevitably found to be inadequate for we cannot describe that which cannot be described.

Out of this non-existence came existence. It came initially as just that, an existence that was totally intangible. We can think of this intangible existence as absolute purity. As this purity is an emanation out of non-existence, we can also think of it as moving and, as it is moving, we can consider it to be a force, a flow of absolute purity. All such concepts are, of course, analogous, but they allow us to have an image that we can use.

Let us continue to use our imagination. Let us perceive a point when the non-existent became aware of the emanation, the pure force, for that awareness created another state of being. This state of being, which is the awareness of the non-existent, is a tangible thing and, because it is a tangible thing, the seeds of form are sown. This is the beginning of time.

Time and form are inextricably linked. Time and manifestation walk hand in hand. They are inseparable and will be so until the end of time.

Time is the first birth. Time is also the first death, for from that point the purity was killed. The process of millions of years had begun, a great cycle of involution and evolution. Some call it the fall and the resurrection, others call it the experience of deity; some regard it to be illusion, others as reality. All are right; it depends upon the way of understanding that pertains in the different schools. All of them are analogous, but all obey the greater laws of nature as known to students of the occult.

Here in the manifest world we use time as a tool and a measure. It is incredibly useful. Scientists and engineers have refined the measure of the earth's journey around the sun to a level of accuracy that is quite remarkable. Its uses in transport, navigation and communication, for example, are many and a valuable benefit to us all.

As students of the occult, we have another concept of time; we are aware of its symbolism and reality in other ways. These ways are symbolised by the Saturnian planetary force. In astrology, Saturn is known as a malefic. This places a limitation upon the planet's influence that is unworthy.

Saturn has many roles. He is the great tester. He is also the guardian of the gate and he is the guide. These roles apply to all walks of life but here we are concerned with the way of initiation and magic.

He is the servant of the Goddess. He understands the mystery of her dark, bitter sea, for it is the price she paid when she gave birth to all. He walks with all in the manifest world and takes their hand each time they cross a threshold by their own free will. He then leads them to the next door and waits, dark and alone, with a patience beyond our imagination.

The glorious days fell.
The dark closed in from each side.
Autumn, then winters night
Lit by noon day light
Borrowed from the summer.

In his hand is the sickle, sometimes the scythe, for he is the harvester. His harvest is selective. He uses the bulk of the grain to make bread and sustain life, but he uses the finest seeds to sow again and improve the quality of the crop. He leads the way on the slow and hard won journey to perfection; the completion of the cycle of millions of years.

Saturn is the measurer in the service of deity and every step of the way will be measured. There are no short cuts. Saturn is the first and the last that we will encounter on our journey

A DIALOGUE

"Rest ye not here, move on."

"But I am sore and weary."

"Rest ye not here, move on."

"But I have struggled long, a little rest cannot be wrong."

"Move on for time is inert. A rest here will not refresh."

"If time is inert, I will sleep on its still bed."

"Move on."

"My limbs resist."

"Move on."

"Time, comfort me."

"Move on and I will give you rest; and my rest will renew."

"I move my sluggish limbs, I strive. I tempt the unknown."

"I am the dread Lord of Shadows, my rest will revive."

"Now I see."

"Verily. Out of darkness cometh light. Move on."

SOME CAUTIONARY WORDS

The measure of time that we use in our earthly world is based upon observations of the turning earth and its journey around the sun.

However, timescales differ in different worlds or states of being, or dimensions or whatever term applies to a persons understanding.

In another place and time lived lost Atlantis.
In our time lives the influence of lost Atlantis.

In a magical work the practitioner uses or influences the forces behind manifestation. To do this, in one way or another, a link must be made with the inner worlds. Once this link is made, the earthly concept of time no longer exists. It matters not whether the work is of an earthly nature, or of a mystical nature, or of any other. Once the work is done it should be allowed to take its own time to come to completion, no matter how long that may be, for we must always work with nature. There are those who include within their work a timetable for its completion. The achievement of this timescale comes at a price, however, because nature is being "forced" to bring on the outcome. The bow wave created by this forcing will leave its mark. You have been given sound advice.

SOME HEARTENING WORDS

Saturn is the dark one. His role in ensuring that the experience of deity is eventually fulfilled may be outwardly disturbing, but inwardly it is driven towards perfection, for nothing can return to the original purity until it is worthy. This message is given in so many ways. Let each find their own.

Saturn and time are one, but ultimate wisdom is timeless. It is beyond silence and it is only seen before the Mighty One.

7

THE EIGHT FESTIVALS – A MAGICAL PERSPECTIVE

Most modern pagan communities relate in one way or another to the eight festivals of the year. The history of these festivals has been extensively researched and from this research a mix of fact, speculation and diverse interpretation has been laid before us. It must be made clear that it is not the intention of this paper to offer a new authentic guide, for in truth, it has little concern with any of these historic details. Nor do these words concern themselves with the various names applied to each one, be it Candlemas or Imbolc, Halloween or Samhain, Christmas or Yule and so on unless there is a positive symbolic reason for their use. The festivals are the festivals. They are points on the wheel of the year and they are there for all, be they Pagans, Christians, secular celebrants or any other. Our concern here is purely with the esoteric aspects as perceived and used by magical practitioners.

To a practitioner of esoteric magic, there are forces in nature, and it should be noted that nature has a far greater meaning to such a practitioner, for it is the Logos made manifest. These tides and forces are there to be used as part of the evolutionary cycle and the points on the wheel of the year that we call the festivals are a symbolic focus of these powerful forces.

As already mentioned, the festivals are there for all. For example, they will have meaning for the astrologer and the astronomer as well as the meteorologist and the farmer. They are also key points on the calendar for both the Christian and the Pagan. In addition, there will be those who just want to get together with like-minded people to party on one of these dates. Christmas and New Year is a good example of this. There will be those who want to visit an ancient monument and see the sun rise to mark a solstice or equinox because they too regard this to be an opportunity to celebrate. If such celebrations are taken for what they are, and that is entertainment, so be it. But let it not be confused with or carried out in the dubious guise of some great ancient mystical enterprise, for that is illusion.

The reality of these markers on the journey of our planet around the sun is that they are not eternally fixed. Just like the stars in the heavens, they will one day be deceivers. The central star of old was not Polaris. Nor will Polaris be the central star of the future. The demons of today are often the great gods of yesterday. But great they were. They symbolised a living truth in their time and the wise were able to work with the forces that they represented, seeing them as an evolving living influence.

Here is a wheel of the year of Goddess and God.

> She is one and She is many
> And He is Her only son.
> At the promise of winters nearing end
> He kicks and runs from Her care.
> Now wild is He but never free
> For She draws Him in with Her thread of love.
> The choice is not His.
> No longer the Mother,
> Now His only lover.
> Enraptured He gives His all.
> Wild are They in ecstasy.
> They lead the May.
> The madness of that rampant day
> And, in glory, He climbs unto the heavens
> Drawn by Her arching body
> As it spans the firmament.
> She is Whole.
> Her benevolence is upon us,
> For great is the Mother Who givest all.
> She spans the void and the earth is filled with Her bounty.
> She is ever living,
> But He must die, and She cries those bitter tears.
> Wrapped in Her loving arms He bares the seed within.
> He takes it to the darkest place
> And rests in perfect peace.
> 'Twas by Her grace He reigned
> And 'tis by Her grace He will reign again
> And Her son, the sun, is born anew
> At the turning of the year.

Anyone with sensitivity will feel the influence of the changing seasons. Not just by being aware of what is happening now, but also feeling the poignancy of what has gone entwined with the potential of what is to come. For changing seasons are a living, evolving process.

The practitioners of esoteric magic will be even more aware of these changes. They will know of the forces that drive the ever-changing year, for they are written into the way of magic. They have been observed and used by students of the occult for many years. With skill and proven techniques they are able to influence these forces so that they can be used to power their chosen work. For them there is no point in ritually celebrating any of the eight festivals unless there is a purpose and the purpose should be a work of light that will play its part in driving the wheel forward. As each festival approaches, the practitioner will consider its worth. The question will be asked, "Can this tide be used?" If it is so the appropriate work will be prepared. The method will be based on a firm foundation steeped in tradition in the classic sense, for the ways are tried and tested. The work itself will be based on that which has been done before, albeit but a few days ago or even a thousand years ago. It matters not so long as it is a genuine progression.

Many will know that the eight festivals of the year are made up of two sets of four.

> How vast is the chariot of the gods?
> Its canopy is the heavens.
> Duality is its power.
> Two sphinxes, one black, one white.
> Two serpents, one winged, one not.
> As the four spoked wheels turn,
> The axis moves,
> The triumph of the light.

It is right to use the seasons, the festivals, the spokes of the earthly wheel to progress the great work. As above, so below and as below, so above. The time will eventually come when the patterns change and new foundations evolve. Until that time the initiate will use the forces that exist knowing that they have their place, but also knowing that they are never an end in themselves. False gods are easy to find.

Here are a few words for each of the eight festivals. Please make of them what you will.

Ride, ride Beltane's tide, harness in hand, strong in the land, use its fire, use its life, use it well and feed it well.

Clear is my sight, clear is my eye, glorious light that one day will die. Remember these times; remember them well. Return them three fold in the dark that will come.

The sacrifice is willingly made. The seed is now within; the promise fulfilled.

For gladly is the journey made in the knowledge that the seed will be reborn. But never forget that the sacrifice is real.

Thin is the veil this night. Blessed are the waiting, and blessed are we in the knowledge of the spirit eternal. Let us give thanks to those who led the way.

I cleanse you of all you know and send you back anew. Within you will be my light. Take it and by your own free will spread its glory. A birth.

I've sown the seeds of life and death. I've sown them in Her winter's breath. Some will live and some will die. But all will be reaped one day.

As the bride of spring and her consort cast their blessing upon the earth, Let us exercise our right to quicken the coming of the light, for we are priestesses and priests.

As already mentioned, the festivals are there for all and may everyone find what they seek, be they pilgrims, holidaymakers, initiates, gardeners or any others who feel an affinity.

But for those who choose to influence the hidden forces it is right to mention that it can only be done by an act of giving. This law applies to all.

8

THE LEGEND OF A WITCH NAME

Falling, tumbling, ever descending.
Endless visions and places.
Falling through worlds of never ending,
Of fabulous beasts and graces.

Falling, falling………………………..

The dreamer wakes in morning cold
As sleep takes its bow.
The heaviness of earth takes hold.
Lost the solemn vow.
Clothed in many colours, he rises,
Familiar sights he'll find.
Nothing new, nothing surprises,
The wonders are far behind.
Lost are the wonders for this incarnation,
Lost are the plan and the reason.
He'll find them anew without explanation
For right are the place and the season.

"What is your name?" calls a voice from on high.
"It's in the plan", he replies.
"What is your name?"
"I am a man"
"What is your name?"
"I cannot remember."
"Find your name, rekindle the ember."
"I have no name."

"You are a confused dreamer, begin with 'Red Mare.'"

Red Mare dwelt among the ones
Who lived from this fine soil.
With mothers, fathers, daughters and sons
He shared in play and toil.

But as he helped with the seeding and growing
Of the people of this land,
The ember within began a glowing,
He needed a guiding hand.

Alone in the night he called to the light,
"Something unsettles me".
The voice in reply came from on high,
"A name will set you free".

"What is your name?"
"Red Mare."
"It is no more. What is your name?"
"I have no name."
"Then let it be "Eseker"".

Eseker took his name
And travelled as he must
To find a One of ancient fame,
A One whom he could trust.
The ember glowed, kindling hope,
At every door he'd knock.
Yet not guru nor priest nor catholic pope
Held out the key to the lock.
He cried again to the light in the night
And a voice from on high replied,
*"The name that you have is the name that is right,
Use it to find a true guide".*
And in silence and time in the way of the meek,
Humbled by realisation
Eseker lost the reason to seek,
For he knew his magic foundation.

A witch he became, but not of the crowd.
One silent and learned and blessed.
A priest of his craft away from the loud,
With Goddess and God he would rest.

But his guide one day took right away
The comfort that he had found.
She took his name with hand of flame
And threw it to the ground.

"What is your name?" she asked.
"I have no name."
"I give you a new name; tell it to none unless the reason is
pure. Your name is Verres."

There is no rest at the Goddesses' breast
For the servers of Her will.
No place for the showy in self-seeking quest.
'Tis work that will fulfil.

"Tell no one your name unless the reason is pure."

But piety is a terrible thing
That servers must redress
And Verres fell into the gap
'Twixt right and pompousness.
Verres boasted and told of his name
Like others with fancy titles.
With ones that they call lost and profane,
All lengthening the cycles.
His guide with loving scrutiny
Watched the failing one.
Watched his rebellious mutiny
And waited in the sun.

Her sacrifice.

As is the way, there came a day
When Verres woke again
And in his service to Goddess and God
He blessed his given name.
The sacrifice of his patient guide
Took Verres through the maze.
His name was changed to advance the tide,
The ember was now ablaze.
She cast him out, she sent him forth.
"Be gone from me be gone.
Take your new name and use its worth
It is time to journey on".

This time he chose the name himself.
This time his will was strong.

He chose a name of strength and health
For he knew the path was long.

He chose, "Old Cunar".

No one knew of his witch name
Unless in total trust.
But he shared with others his living flame
As sometimes he knew he must.
The many-coloured coat he wore
As he woke upon earth's floor
Carried within it seeds of hope
For the needing at the door.
He sowed the seeds of hope and wonder
Fulfilling of his vow.
He sowed the seeds to few in number,
And left them there to grow.

He gave for 'twas his inspiration
As every name should be.
For a witches name is aspiration,
Not a trinket or mock royalty.
Titles have no place in Her work,
For they belong to another.
Vanity's embellishment
Are a show, a sham, a cover.

Old Cunar found the reason,
The ember a lantern bright.
He rode the tide and used the season
And shared Her loving light.
He poured from the cauldron Her inspiration.
The cauldron of rebirth.
He used his name as true aspiration
To give to those on the earth.

He thought he'd take his name when he
Left this incarnation.
But Old Cunar had ceased to be.
No need for aspiration.

Just blessed rest.

9

LEVELS OF BEING

Practitioners of magic and mysticism recognise the wholeness of nature. They also recognise that this wholeness is, in our terms, infinite.

To be able to acquire a little understanding of this wholeness and work within it, some form of structure is needed. Fortunately, we stand on the shoulders of giants. These structures have been evolved over many years and in many cultures by the great ones who have gone before. It is important to know that these structures are not a reality, or an end in themselves, far from it. They are symbolic. But their symbolism allows the initiates to play their part in the way that they have chosen, for these symbolic structures, used with understanding, are keys that unlock doors that will enable the initiates to work within.

The structures can take many forms. A fine example is Cabala, for it is a superb and all-inclusive system. Students of Cabala can use the tree of life with its ten holy sephiroth and twenty-two paths, or adopt the mystical use of the letters of the Hebrew alphabet, or study the Sepher Zohar and all other illuminating texts.

Another skeleton, or scaffolding, is the sevenfold planetary system or (for those who choose) the same system but with the inclusion of the three later planetary discoveries of Pluto, Uranus and Neptune.

There are also the twin triangles symbolising the reflection that becomes merged in the six-pointed star.

Then there is the excellent pentagram with the four elements of earth, water, air and fire below and spirit at its zenith.

There are others. There are myths and legends, there is the Enochian system as adapted by Liddell Mathers, there is Jacobs ladder, there is the number system of Pythagoras, there is the esoteric tarot, there are systems built around ritual objects such as the chalice or the platter or the flame and so on.

All of these can be used if the practitioners have a proper understanding of their chosen way.

It will be noted that in nearly all of these there is a system of hierarchy or levels of being. This is a device that enables students of the occult to overcome the limitations of the human mind for, as stated at the outset, they have to find a way of dealing with a reality of oneness that is beyond rational thought processes. Occult means hidden and the adopted system must enable the students to explore the hidden parts of the wholeness, for what the students seek is a way to work with those forces that are within, behind and beyond the manifest.

> Locked in stone, foundation's throne
> Established in the earth.
> Upon the stone, upon the throne
> Is where we test our worth.
> From the inner to the outer,
> From darkness to rebirth.

Little by little, the fire that drives the initiates will lead them towards a small understanding of this inner world; an understanding that can rarely be explained but can, sometimes, be shared with like minded people.

This is an opportune place to once again counsel the reader to be wary of the academic rationalist. Such a person will use an extensive vocabulary to eloquently explain the way of the mystic or the magician in pseudo psychological terms. Examples of these explanations are the simple need for escapism, or the need for a father or mother figure, or instability, or fear of physical death and so on. The logic applied by these erudite people is based on their own experience; an experience that lacks the "knowing" that belongs to the initiate. It is also a good opportunity to counsel the reader to be wary of writers on occult matters who also choose to rationalise the teachings. They are imposing their understanding upon the student instead of allowing the student to explore the hidden roads and find their own inner knowing.

Illusion's moon, deceiving ocean,
Can we leave your shore?
Can we control your seething motion
And see wild dreams no more?
Yes.
Build your boat and rule emotion
And work with nature's law.

Levels of being have been introduced into these structures because they give us an insight into the types of influences or forces that exist. They also give us a mountain path that can lead us towards the summit, or centre, or origin, or end, or ....

Let us take as an example the occult elements. Scholars will probably tell us about the origins of this system being found in the writings of Aristotle and they will be right in their terms. However, we are not considering the elements as a history or as an exact science. We are dealing with a symbolic system that can help students and practitioners of magic in their chosen work. The reason that the use of the occult elements endures is because, for many, it works and what better reason can there be.

It is doubtful if any two people will agree about the qualities of the elements, nor does it matter. The variations tend to be subtle and each must come to their own understanding. As stated, this is not a science, as it is generally understood, but a means of accessing the forces behind manifestation.

It is important to keep in mind that in almost all elemental systems, the four elements evolve from a fifth. This fifth is known by many names; it can be called aether, or akasha, or the quintessence, or spirit, etc.

Labour with thoughts, labour with vision.
Twisting serpents and rod.
Develop a way and use with precision,
Bestow the blessings of Hod.
In wisdom's foundation make every decision
In service of Goddess and God.

Most systems will have sub divisions that allow for a greater subtlety. One version is fourfold where each element is influenced by the quality of the others. For example, water would be divided into earth of water, water of water, air of water and fire of water. Also, as stated, we should never forget the fifth, i.e. spirit of water.

The suites of the esoteric tarot provide an excellent system. For there are four suites and fourteen cards to a suite. This gives a total of fifty-six divisions or levels.

There are also the worlds of the elements. Each one has its own geography, flora and fauna. These worlds are inhabited by personifications of what they represent. There are sylphs for air, undines for water, gnomes for earth and salamanders for fire. From the point of view of the practitioner, however, it is not wise to work with these aspects directly. Such work should always be done through the higher rulers of these elemental worlds however they are known.

An excellent way of working is by using elemental symbols in ritual. Earth can be the pentacle, ash, bread or salt. For water there is the cup or bowl. For air, incense and perfumes and for fire the candle or the lantern. It would not normally be necessary to have a symbol for the quintessence.

Reference has been made to rising on the planes and this most certainly can be done. It can be done using the sepherothic system of Cabala with its four worlds. It can be done by making a symbolic journey through a mythical land. It can be done using the elements or by adapting and using any of the other systems alluded to in these writings. If done properly following sound guidance, it works.

> Beyond the flame, the unknown name
> Unspeakable and right.
> Beyond the flame, the silent reign,
> The glory in the night.
> Beyond the flame, beyond the flame,
> Beyond both black and white.

Practitioners should always work at as high a level as they can. The question is why do we do it? Some will say it is for my own spiritual development. The question is then asked, "What do you mean by spiritual development? To what end?" These are important questions, for "navel gazing" and "What's in it for me" form a large part of the public image of magic in these times.

The genuine western schools have clear objectives in mind. A well known one is "We learn in order to serve". Another is "We bring through the light". In other words, each should take that which is earned out into the world in whichever way they are able.

10

INITIATION

Initiation in the wider world is without ambiguity. It happens in factory and office, on farms and in the armed forces, in social groups and in sports clubs. At its best, it is part of a positive learning process and at its worst it is destructive to the persons involved. Whilst recognising the validity of this aspect of initiation, it is not the concern of this book.

In the, so-called, spiritual world there are two distinct ways of understanding. There is the exoteric way of understanding and there is the esoteric way of understanding. This is also true of initiation. There is exoteric initiation and there is esoteric initiation. Many spiritual or magical organisations have initiation rites or ceremonies and, as a general trend, those who seek to spread their understanding of the way to as many people as possible tend to be exoteric. It is a trend that can create a fog of confusion for many a seeker, for these are the organisations most frequently encountered.

This paper is about the way of the few. It is for those people who sooner or later become dissatisfied with the approach of the exoteric groups, for they know that there is something more. Initiation to them is of a different order, far more than a warm glow. What they seek is the inner way, the esoteric way.

> What price initiation?
> What power, what love, what for?
> What price initiation?
> Why enter that dark door?

A call is heard. It comes from somewhere within and from somewhere beyond and both are one and the same, for both are infinite. To respond to this call is a choice of free will, for the response involves the sacrifice of the familiar and outwardly comforting. It is a step into the unknown, an act of courage and trust. It involves a journey into that unknown place and the unknown is always dark; a first step into the cosmos to search for the brightest star. Few really take this first step although many claim to have done so. This is the process of the first initiation.

The decision to initiate lies with the initiator for it is only for those who are ready. It is not a task taken lightly. The door will be opened and it takes the initiate onto a road that cannot be avoided. Once on that road, the initiate may choose to pause, or explore a side road, or rage against the difficulties along the way. The initiate may stumble, deny, laugh or cry. It matters not. Once the first step is taken, lifetime by lifetime, the work of life will be there and its fulfilment will be the only driving force. Stories of the journey abound. There is Jacob's ladder, the holy grail, Dante, the pearl of great price, the quest of the alchemist, and so on. All are symbols of the way.

Knowing how to recognise a genuine guide and initiator is an eternal dilemma for the seeker and there are no easy answers. Here are a few of the well-documented warnings that can be found in the more reliable publications.

Be wary of fancy dress. If they "look the part" it often means that they need the trappings to compensate for a lack of substance. Be wary of requests for money other than a minimal sum to cover necessary expenses. You cannot buy or sell spirituality or magic. Be wary of promises such as, revealing the mysteries, or giving you great powers, or putting you in contact with great entities, or solving your personal problems, and so on. Be particularly wary if they offer these things in a very short space of time. Be wary of claims of endless success and of having multitudes of adoring followers. Be wary of those who tell you what you want to hear instead of what you need to hear. There are other warning signs, but this will suffice for our purposes.

Here are some of the elements that make up an initiation ceremony or ritual. The place must be properly prepared. In whatever form it takes, it will be a temple and the initiation will take place under the authority of the highest. There is usually a challenge and a warning; a test of the sincerity and courage of the postulant. There is often an oath of secrecy, a way of making sure that the postulant knows that the path is for the few, that it is not to be dissipated and trivialised by public show and display. The postulants may be asked if they are prepared to undergo a ritual form of suffering; for nothing worthwhile ever comes easy. It will be by their own efforts that anything will be achieved. The way of the initiate is far more than an academic course of study with a diploma at the end. Recognition of achievement will be in the heart. There may be an anointing, as these are holy commitments. There will be an introduction to the great ones of the inner planes in whichever way they are perceived.

The ones who have gone before and go before clear away the mists from the places where others are now able to go, but all else remains hidden. Their work goes on. They will choose those among us who can help in this work, but they cannot make us do it or make it easy for us to do. It has to be by our own will and our own efforts.

There may be further warnings. Most importantly, the question will be asked, "What are you prepared to give?"

Rest assured, in a true initiation, the person who asks, "What's in it for me?" will not be accepted as an initiate.

Initiation is sometimes called, "The greater death", for the commitment is an eternal one. It is based on the law of sacrifice, a sacrifice to the greater work in the way that it is understood by each school, for they know that in the end, all the ways are one way.

> I am what I am to be.
> The eye of truth is penetrating me.
> Transparent before the mighty three,
> My Goddess, My God,
> Eternity.

Initiation is not just one ceremony or even a series of ceremonies leading to higher and higher grades, although these have their place. Initiation is a continuous process of death and birth in all its myriad forms and to the true initiate, there will never be any doubt about its rightness.

Once the initiation has taken place, the initiates will find opportunities to learn and advance the work put before them. They may also find themselves confronted by personal issues that have not been successfully addressed in their lives. This is a common occurrence and it is expected because the very act of initiation sets in motion a process that hastens karma. These events soon dispel any doubts about the validity of the initiation. The role of the dark one, the tester, becomes a conscious part of the initiate's life. This should be welcomed, for the tester is also the guide who will both guard and show the way.

Let us dispel any illusions that may exist about the fatality of initiation. Nothing and no one, no matter how great, no matter how holy, no matter if it is deity itself can take away the free will of the initiate (or anybody else for that matter). Guidance may be given, but all actions, all decisions, all words spoken, etc. are entirely the responsibility of the initiate.

In this world the way of initiation can be a lonely one. Like the hermit in the tarot pack who holds his light before him, it is held in the hands of the initiates and by their own efforts they walk their chosen path. It may sound harsh and relentless. It is not.

We all know the famous names of history, Rudolph Steiner, Helena Petrovna Blavatsky, Dion Fortune, Jacob Bohme, Robert Fludd, Eliphas Levi, Abraham Abulafia and so on. We are grateful for all that they have put before us. But we must never forget the majority who chose to play their part in silence, humility and obscurity, leaving their mark without a name. This they did willingly because true initiates know that their work is genuinely fulfilling and in that they will never be alone.

11

THE MAGIC LOOP

A magical process can be thought of as a loop. Paradoxically it is a loop that is never completely joined. The paradox continues for, although it is never completely joined, it is none the less endless in any terms that we can understand.

A fine example of a magic loop is the ouroboros, the serpent devouring its own tail. Much can be gleaned from this image for it is ancient and has been consistently used by the wise as a potent symbol.

Let us take a simple interpretation. As the serpent devours its own tail it is also rotating, moving forwards. It is feeding upon its own experience, learning thereby and evolving. It is doing this by its own efforts and by its own will. As it is constantly evolving, it never succeeds in devouring itself. Therefore the loop cannot be completed.

In this process we find many of the basic components that go into the creative act of magic. For example, using experience and hard won ability, making a point of learning from each experience, (There is only one test of magic, does it work?), moving in a forward direction even though it is in the form of a loop and doing this by ones own effort and will. The more that is put into the process, the better will be the results. If the process is truly one of evolution, then the whole of the serpent will rise to a higher level of being, but based on a very firm foundation; a foundation that is built as it evolves. Many of you will say that this also applies to life, and so it does.

An act of magic adapts nature by using nature's forces, for no one, not even the greatest of magical practitioners, can work against the laws of nature. In our representation, we will consider nature to be made up of myriads of loops. There is the cycle of life, death and birth. There is the journey from seed to plant to fruit and back to a newly evolved seed. There is the wheel of the heavens. In the world of magic, these can be symbolically represented as the wheel of fortune, the four occult elements, Tetragrammaton (yod, he, vau, he), the magic circle and so on.

All of these loops are part of one infinitely vast loop.

Loving couples are a fine example of small loops and each of these couples will be made up of many more small loops. The most potent and well known of these loops is the living polarity between them where the woman is positive in the head and stimulates the man. She does this in a host of different ways; a stimulation that he accepts passively in his head. This potency is then shown in the phallus and the loving woman, when ready, becomes receptive. This loop is used deliberately in all walks of life, for the potency engendered in the man is not only shown in the phallus. The stimulus is also a driving force for a host of other activities, thereby creating or using other loops.

Let us return to the way of magic. There are very basic forms of magic. They can be in the form of spells, or in the use of talismans, or in the use of prayers and so on.

We will take a very simple prayer as an example, a plea to deity for help. It matters not whether the prayer is a selfish desire, or a call for help for a needy person, or to end a war, or to take away troubles, etc. In all of these cases the person praying is calling on their deity to intervene. It has already been stated that no one can work against nature. To have a reaction, there must be an action. Because the prayer is little more than a pleading in the hope of intervention, the action on the part of the person praying is minimal and there will not be the desired outcome, only the status quo, which will evolve in its own way. The same failure will apply to people who make simple spells with little or no understanding of what they are doing or of the need to make it happen.

Once in a while (though rarely) the current started by one of these prayers or simple spells does get picked up by a loop and an outcome similar to the one requested eventually transpires. Because the person who initiated the work made no real effort towards the outcome, other than a request or an incantation with an intent, the loop that was used had to find a way to extract the energy or force needed for it to evolve. This is usually taken from the person who started the process in one form or another. In nature, everything has its price and, if the dues are not paid in advance, they will be collected later. Disruption in the life of the person involved is the way normally observed. Wishful thinking is not magic. There are sound rules to a magical process and a way must always be found to pay in advance.

It is with good reason that the great writers on the western way of magic use such terms as, "enflame yourself with prayer". Make your sacrifice real. This can take many forms. If we look to other cultures and watch the magical or mystic person at work, we will observe everything from dramatic frenzy to long periods of isolation in a desolate place. There may be an act of physical giving or an arrow of focussed emotional power brought on by deliberate stimulation. The principle is the same, only the methods differ. It should be done in the way that has been taught after proper preparation, thereby ensuring safety to the operator and purity of intent. A wonderful example of preparation for a great magical work is given in the way of Abramelin the Mage where months of purification and devotion are necessary before the results can be achieved. There are many examples of people who suffered because they practised this way without the necessary preparation.

Those who practice the inner way of magic, the esoteric way, find that they become less and less involved in earth magic. Such acts usually conflict with karmic law and are mostly involved in dealing with symptoms or effects, not causes. Their approach is of another order.

> Think not of distance.
> Think not of time.
> Think in another way,
> Transcendent, sublime.

Their work is still involved with influencing the manifest, but they know that it is a work of millions of years. They also know that they must work with nature under the highest authority, deity or the cause of causes in whichever way it is conceived. Whenever a work is done, they must be able to say, "May my will be Thy will". This does not take away their responsibility. On the contrary, it recognises a greater responsibility, the need to do that which is right as opposed to that which is desirable. They are ever aware that each time they use or create a loop that influences the manifest, it must also be a blessed influence to the greater loop, the great wheel, the wheel of involution and evolution. This is why loops cannot be closed, for to try to close a loop creates inertia and that inertia has to be broken by an act of destruction; Martian force in the service of deity.

Allegorical descriptions of the great loop can be found in esoteric writings such as, "The Secret Doctrine" by Helena Petrovna Blavatsky or, "The Cosmic Doctrine" by Dion Fortune. They can also be found in expressions such as, "The one from whom all things proceed and into whom all things must return".

To bring through a work, it is necessary to create a space in manifestation. The practitioner, or the working group, creates the space by giving to the highest. The gift can then be transmuted and returned. Those with open eyes will see in this method a magical loop. They will also see that it is used with the greater loop in mind.

Practitioners of the western way often describe their work as "bringing through the light". It is as good an explanation as any other.

12

THE CHALICE

The chalice is a symbol, not an object of veneration. It matters not how it is made, whether it be of silver, or of gold, or of wood. It matters not whether it is superbly engraved with intricate designs or encrusted with the rarest of jewels. If it is a physical thing, it is right that it should be made with love and respect; also that it should be properly consecrated and dedicated. But it must never be venerated as an object in itself. This false veneration is superbly illustrated in *War in Heaven* by Charles Williams.

As already stated, it is a symbol and it is one of the finest of symbols.

Over the years, a great deal has been written about the chalice, volumes of useful information about its symbolism. It can be the receptive principle, the feminine, the cauldron of Cerridwen, the cornucopia, the well, the eternal spring, the grail of the last supper, for instance. This information will not be repeated and elaborated upon in these writings. Instead, what follows is a series of scenarios that can be used for contemplation and meditation if they are found to be worthy or resonate with the reader.

*

The waters are still. They know not heat, nor cold, nor new, nor old. These may be the primordial waters, or the waters of the daughter who is also the Great Mother. So vast are they and so far away, it is almost impossible to tell. Both are emanations. Both have names given to those in contemplation and given by them to every nation.

*

"Why this empty space? Why this blessed grace?" the students ask in their heightened awareness. And a dark one says, "Leave selfish dreams behind. Make the grace solid. Make it live. Tread it well into the earth where root and branch will flourish and new seeds will be cast forth." "How?" they ask and the dark one says, "By the ways you have been taught."

*

Another sits at the wellhead. The heat of the sun is upon her and upon the wellhead, but the waters are cool and refreshing in the darkness below. For the heat of the sun and the cool of the water is a blessed combination and she is near to their point of union.

*

We will be the fire that heats the cauldron. Most will come, drink all that they see and move on. But some will sip and realise its infinite vastness, and stay.

*

Empty hands are a cup that can be filled. What they can be filled with is "in the hands" of the receiver. The hands are also used for doing and giving. What should be received in the cupped hands? How shall it be given? How shall it be done?

*

With a different eye he looked to the west as the sun slowly descended into the still waters of the ocean. Together, sun and ocean faded into night and will never rise again in the west. What is the mystery of this union? It is not the same sun that rises anew in the east. The one that slowly descended into Her welcoming arms was spent, for it had given all. It is a seemingly miraculous transformation.

*

The flowing stream is crystal clear .On the opposite bank she sits on a throne of stone resplendent in blue and white. Her face is a hidden mystery as it ever was and is and ever shall be. Resting upon her lap is a silver chalice. She is waiting.

*

With roots firmly planted in the earth, the water lily rises through the watery realm and rests upon its surface. The water is its servant and, in the air above, it opens its many petalled white flower to the light of the sun. As should we.

*

Cast the circle; cast it well.
Cast the circle; invert the bell.
Fill it with wine
From a hand that is ready,
Whilst held in another
Waiting and steady.
Fire it with power,
The power of creation.
Then lovingly share
This blessed libation.

*

If you gaze into the fountain to see what you want to see, it will be there. Illusory.

If you gaze into the fountain to see what is really there, another eye is opened. Not immediately, but when ready, and then, only little by little; for our lives are as a string of pearls at the throat of the Goddess and this is but one of them.

*

The curved bowl cannot stand firmly upon the earth. It is unbalanced. A foursquare base maintains its place.

Most find four the best.

To lift the bowl takes two .Two handles and also two hands; one hard and one soft; one from the day and one from the night; one from the earth and one in flight; for from opposite horizons they must come, and come together in harmony.

*

The mystery of the waters is to be found in its depth, not in its turbulence.

*

The students asked (or told) the wise one,

"Let us have beautiful music to help us in our work. Sounds that are bewitching and melodies that linger. A mood set by an enriched sound can lead to the meaningful and the profound".

The wise one replied,

"Music and sounds have their place, but do not fear the silence. Do not shy away and seek the comforting noises that are so familiar, for they will bar the way. A fear of silence is a fear of being alone, but in perfect silence you cannot be alone".

Some will listen.

Some will seek the silence.

13

MORE THAN A WORD

In the world of esoteric magic a word will often take on a special significance. A practitioner will refer to the word (the logos), or use a word of power. A word can be a magical name, or it can be a visualised word, or a sound, or a written word, or a secret word, and so on.

A little study will reveal that the word or the logos is used to describe the creative act in various ways in a number of cultures throughout the world. This is a deep well of mystery for those who are prepared to contemplate its meaning. Although what follows will be focussed upon the use of words in the practice of esoteric magic, this creative word will remain firmly within our awareness for magic works with the cause, not the effect.

> The first word is a sound;
> From where, who can tell?
> The second sound is all of the words,
> But what are the sounds in between?

Let us begin by considering magical alphabets, or more accurately, alphabets used in magic, for the written word is always constructed from the letters of an alphabet. A well-known example of a word used in magic is the all-encompassing "Azoth". It is a word made up of a combination of the first and last letters of three alphabets, Hebrew, Greek and English. It is all embracing and has special significance for those who understand the way to use these alphabets.

An alphabet used magically translates each letter into a series of symbols, or values. An example, in the western mystery tradition, would be the Hebrew letter, "vau". This letter represents a nail or a peg, it has a numerical value of six, its astrological correspondence is Taurus and its tarot correspondence is the Hierophant. Other correspondences will evolve with experience and use, for example the shape or form of the letter may have meaning for the user, or there could be a colour association and so on. There is no limit.

These symbols, to a certain extent, rationalise a system. But do mark the words, "to a certain extent". Magic is not an exact science that can be explained away so easily as so many would like to be able to do. These values and symbols are triggers or keys; they are not "painting by numbers".

It does not take a massive leap of imagination to see that a combination of these letters put together can create a word that has a particular meaning, a word that can be used in a magical operation to help achieve the right process. A word that appears utterly meaningless to the casual reader takes on an altogether different nature when the reader realises the rich symbolism that it contains. For much deliberation on the part of the user will have gone into the construction of what appears to be a nonsensical word to those who are unfamiliar with the inner way.

The numerical value of letters has been mentioned above. The Hebrew practitioners of Cabala are probably the finest exponents of working with these numerical values and a study of Gematria on the part of the reader is well worthwhile. Used correctly, the chains of correspondences created by this number system can lead to fresh insights on the part of the practitioner that other processes clearly fail to achieve; an excellent use of words using a magical system.

As we are discussing the use of words in Hebrew Cabala, it is also a good opportunity to mention the Cabalistic technique of visualising words in a particularly powerful form of meditation. In this form, a series of letters (which must, by its nature, be a word or series of words) is visualised by the person meditating. The words are held strongly in vision by the power of a constructive imagination. With great skill they are observed, rotated and permutated until, eventually, they open the door to another way of seeing.

Whilst not trying to emulate this disciplined and highly evolved system, it is a fascinating practice for anyone, magician or not, to dwell upon a word that has meaning for a period of time. The person doing so will, eventually, find that it loses its meaning, that its shape becomes unfamiliar even though it has not changed. An awareness of the spaces between the letters may occur and what is left is a feeling that is somewhat disconcerting; a feeling that takes away the initial certainty that the word held. Perhaps it was the observation of this process that evolved into the controlled systems that are used in magical work.

When the practitioner has an understanding of all the symbolic meaning that goes into a written word, its presentation becomes a magical act. It may be used on a talisman, or as a carefully crafted glyph using an artistic representation of the letters. It may be contained within a planetary square or used in a meditation. Such a word becomes a tool that will help to cultivate the fields prepared by practitioners of esoteric magic in their efforts to reap a finer grain.

> A harvest of words.
> Here is the harvest,
> Scattered in the wind,
> Gathered up in a swirl of air
> And laid at our feet.

Secrecy in magic is frowned upon by many who do not understand its purpose. It is not that the magician chooses to hide great revelations from other people. It is often, simply, that the secrecy itself is a part of the process. If a word is used, it must retain its potency and power. It must be focussed and directed. The word is personal to the practitioner or group of practitioners and it is a simple magical law that to break this secrecy will result in the failure of the work. Another expression of those wise words of Thrice Greatest Hermes, "To know, to dare, to will, to keep silent".

Words can also be expressed spiritually in ritual poses or in dance. A fine example of this method is to be found in the teachings of Rudolf Steiner, or, more accurately, Marie Steiner, who evolved and taught the system of eurythmy. The practice of incorporating a series of movements into a magical work to enhance the power of a word is an excellent thing to do. But it must achieve its objective, i.e. enhance the power. More often than not such movements tend to distract because they are not properly focussed; they are not naturally driven from within. A mechanical act is not a magical act.

Let us move on to the spoken word; mantras, chants, words of power, barbarous names, etc.

The method of repetition using mantras is well known and its effect upon the person, or people, participating is adequately described by masters of the systems that use them. There is little that can be usefully added here.

Words of power and barbarous names are of a different order. Both are voiced, but not as a trained theatrical technique. The way of calling on forces using words of power are described in books but the actual act is far more than this. The real call comes from the depths of the operator's soul; it is indescribable; it is a vibration that resonates not only through the person who is voicing the word but also through all that is around that person; truly a call to the far corners of the universe. It is also a reciprocal process. And to those who state that this is a melodramatic overstatement, the writer replies, experience will show you otherwise.

What words are these?
I do not understand them.
They have no name around them.
They have no soul to ground them.

Sometimes, in a properly built temple, in a state of perfect trust under the authority of the highest, words are given. Some are but sounds. Sounds that penetrate. Sounds that find their way into all of the hidden places that we find so hard to reach. These sounds may shake or loosen, awaken or enlighten, uplift or humble, or still or energise.

Other given words can be most specific and others perplexing.

But all of them are precious gifts to be studied, analysed, meditated upon and, when ready, used wisely.

14

THE CROWN

Magical language is read on many levels. To take it literally would be a misunderstanding, yet to treat it as a work of fiction would be to deny its worth. It is, most certainly, symbolic. When used with knowledge and ability it opens up channels to another way of understanding. Of course, this is not an instant process. It takes time, often a very long time.

You will not find the words that follow informative in the literal sense, nor are they rational in the scientific sense, far from it. They are words written in the way of magic. Please make of them what you will.

From out of "that which cannot be" came pure, pure brilliance contained within a point. Some will say it is Caph, Tau, Resh. Others will say it is the point that is both within and beyond as well as being without centre or boundary. Others will say it is the Aleph, or the first number where all numbers are one. Its first manifestation is infinity and the infinite form it takes is a circle for it is without beginning or end. A circle beyond and beyond. A circle of pure brilliance. A circle that is the crown of crowns. There cannot be any higher. Nor, at its making, could the crown of crowns be known for there were none to know.

When the essence of the crown of crowns descended, some came to know. When the essence of the crown of crowns ascends, all will come to know.

Pure brilliance also became a flame. The flame became the many. The many let go and moved through the worlds created by the non-existent.
Each one of the many hid the flame within, hidden even from themselves. It was lost in the letting go. It was lost in the going out. Lost.

There is the crown of crowns and there is the flame. The crown of crowns sits in glory before that which cannot be. The flame is lost.

The non-existent waits, the crown of crowns at the final gate, the flame lost in the worlds created by the non-existent. All have expectation, an expectation of enriched perfection. It is an evolution.

There is an attraction, a pull. It is so powerful that for this evolution it is a law. This is the law.

The flame must become enriched by experience and join the crown of crowns whilst the crown of crowns must call in the flame.

The hidden flame is working even though most are not aware of the process. The process was and is chaotic, for the world created by the non-existent is all that is known. It is the manifest world and it is a place full of wonder. Only the dreamer or the escapist can deny its reality, or its history, or its future. From the awe inspired by the limitless space that is the universe to the six legged crawling thing upon the earth. From the joy of fleeting happiness to the awful consequences of utter destruction, be it through geological forces or the actions of those who dwell therein. From the genius of considered knowledge to the raw instincts of survival, and so on. Here, in the manifest world created by the non-existent, is experience. Here is karma. Here is the place of enrichment.

The flame alive within, but hidden, the crown of crowns waiting.

A time eventually came in the long lost past when rare ones began to feel and see in another way from those with whom they dwelt. Just a few of them. They were the strange ones in the land. They felt the flame within and questioned its purpose. They were but one or two individuals in different places and cultures. Mostly they were alone and unable to tell anyone of what they began to perceive. Few they were and they were as lost as any others, for the world created by the non-existent is as much a challenge to those who are aware as it is to any other. This they knew, but they also knew that they had found a purpose to their lives and all that was around even though they could not understand and could not explain. Their work began.

This was the time when the crown of crowns sent out an essence of itself into the world created by the non-existent. Although it was just an essence of the crown of crowns, it was an infinite wonder to the bearers of the flames. It took many forms and could be seen or felt in many ways when the eye and heart was open.

The essence of the crown of crowns has nothing to do with the crowns that belong to the world created by the non-existent. These are no better than false copies. They represent ennoblement of self, power by conquest, queens and kings of earthly things, no matter whether they inherit their crowns or whether they are given, whether they are elected or whether they are figureheads. Whether they are self appointed or appointed by their concept of god. They are false crowns. A crown upon the earthly head is a crown of thorns. Real crowns are above the head, not on it. They symbolise aspiration, not the ennoblement of self.

The essence of the crown of crowns took nobler forms. In duality it became Goddess and God. For others it became a trinity. It can be found in heavenly deities symbolised by the sun or the moon or the stars. It is the philosopher's stone. It is the throne chariot of God, the Merkabah. It is the way of the four holy beasts or the elements. It is the many paths of seven encountered in different forms. It is the sacred cup, the grail. It is the pearl of great price. In this way and in many other ways did the essence of the crown of crowns descend.

In order to return to the non-existent, the flame and the crown of crowns must unite in enriched perfection, a process of millions of years. All that are in existence will play their part for there are many ways. Ours is the way of esoteric magic.

We have reached an age when many more can feel and see in that other way. Most will not pursue or realise their potential for to do so is an act of free will and the desire and drive must come from within. Others with fine aspirations will get lost in the mazes put before them in the world created by the non-existent. It is, deliberately, a difficult path, for it is the way of the priest of the sun, the way of sacrifice.

I was taken by the hand and led into a land not of my choosing. A descent if you like, but not a falling. Crowded by the gross, or its images. Untouched by them for I have trust and I trust that the trust I have touched them. My understanding is dim, but when I worked within I tried to take Her light to the ones who've lost the sight of the one who sent us forth. That is work and I was not alone.

As the essence of the crown descended deeper into matter, it picked up the influence of the world created by the non-existent. It became outwardly tarnished. It descended to the black cubical altar and there it rests. It has rested there for thousands of years and will be there for thousands of years to come.

The black cubical altar is matt in colour, for it does not reflect any light. It is made of the densest, darkest and heaviest material that can be known.

Even though the crown that rests upon it is tarnished, to those in manifestation it glows with a brilliant golden light. In legend many have come to this altar. They will not see the crown, only its glory. Some will see a chalice, some only the brilliant light, some a cross, some a star in the night. None of them will have found this altar without the most perilous of quests and, even as they kneel before it, they may well be turned away. Their only measure is the gift that they bring to illuminate the crown. A selfish desire for spiritual attainment alone will not enrich perfection.

We have chosen the inner way, the way of magic. When used by those who are able it works. If the work is right and leads to a good end it will bring a drop of light to the crown upon the black cubical altar. Then the flame and the crown of crowns will become a little closer in a journey of millions of years.

For by our deeds will we be known, not by our desires.

15

THE IMPORTANCE OF PREPARATION

To some the words that follow will be regarded as stating the obvious and they are right. Yet they cannot be repeated too many times.

A need arises. For our purposes, it does not matter what that need might be. What does matter is that a work of magic is conceived as the way to deal with that need. The decision to carry out the work of magic is one of free will on the part of the practitioner. The rightness is not in doubt for, before making the decision, all other options will have been considered. The use of magic is rarely the first choice in these matters for there is usually a better way of fulfilling a need. Patently, it is easier to cultivate a garden using thought, spade, fork and a little muscle power than to conceive a complex magical route that will, eventually, achieve the same result. How ridiculous it is to believe that magic requires less effort and comes without a price. Alas, so many do. Magic is usually used only when all other options have been discarded.

The magician will also have thought long and hard about the karmic repercussions of this action before coming to a decision.

Also, the magician will know that the outcome will be successful, for there cannot be any doubt in the use of esoteric magic. If there is doubt, it will not work.

Once the decision is taken, the process of preparation begins. In this case it has been decided that the work is to be done as the key part of a ritual. Nothing is left to chance and nothing is done casually, for the magician will be harnessing and influencing the forces behind manifestation, the place of the cause, not the symptom. After contemplation and, if possible, consultation with those who guide, the magician will design the ritual. It will be committed to paper and will be complete.

The ritual will include a properly constructed temple. A temple built in such a way that it will become "A place between the worlds" where the inner plane forces can be contacted and influenced. It will be a temple of the highest, of Deity, for we must always work under the highest authority. It will be cleansed and purified for it will be properly protected from all external influences; there must not be anything that can distract the focussed concentration of the magical practitioner who can then work in a state of perfect trust. The ritual will be focussed upon the work to be done and it must be firmly established within the process. The ritual will include a means of ensouling the work to be done. The rule is simple. The amount of energy, or effort, or power required to complete the work is no different from the amount that would be needed if it were being done in any other way. The magician has to know how to charge the work with this power and how to set the work free so that it can complete its task.

The ritual will also include a proper closing at its end.

A time and day will be selected for the work to be done using whatever influence is available to pick the best moment. This can be driven by anything from the urgency created by the need to the complexities of a cosmic timetable. It matters not how it is selected, only that it works.

From the point where the need for the work was considered and up to the point of its completion, concentration will be all-important. Concentration forms a major part of magical ability. This focussed concentration is applied to every aspect; the writing of the ritual is a time of supreme concentration, as is the contemplation, meditation and consultation that will enable the magician to create a formula that will achieve the desired outcome. This same concentration will apply during the days leading up to the work as the magician establishes within a frame of mind that is needed.

A place for the work will be chosen and cleansed in readiness. On the day of the ritual, in this selected place, all the material things that are to be used will be put in their places, but only those items that are to be used and no more. Each item will have a purpose and the magician will know why it is there, for all of these symbolic objects must live. Colours, incense, weapons, words, etc; all must be right, consecrated and dedicated.

What is being created is a temple, for as already mentioned, a chosen work of esoteric magic is a work of Deity and is done under the authority of the highest that can be. All else is dabbling.

Let us not at any point forget that all of this is being done with a focussed concentration.

The preparation of the magician is all-important. The intake of food is controlled. This can vary from fasting to doing enough to ensure that the gripes of the body do not disturb the progress of the work.

There is also ritual cleansing. This is both a mental and physical process. This process of purity of intent will have begun when the work was conceived. The magician must become a fit person to carry out the work, a person who is able to stand in the temple and be completely transparent before the Deity, for there cannot be anything to hide or any hidden agendas. Achieving this purity can be aided by ritual bathing prior to the work.

A wonderful example of focus and preparation is given in "The Book of the Sacred Magic of Abramelin the Mage". In this case the preparation is spread over many months and it is clearly stated that the work cannot be achieved without this tremendous discipline.

Returning to our own work, the preparation must be appropriate to the operation and each will decide as to what is right for, rest assured, a casual approach will achieve the result it merits. You have been advised. Also, there is no substitute for ability and, in this respect, magic differs not one jot from any other walk of life.

The magician may choose to work robed or without clothes of any kind, i.e. sky clad. If the latter way is chosen, then it will be a beautiful expression of trust and transparency in the presence of the highest.

If the magician is to be robed, then the robe selected will be appropriate. It may be one that is plain and sombre in colour symbolising humility and diligence. It may be one of a particular colour that is suitable for the operation, or it may have symbolic additions that are also suitable. What it must not be is a glorified embellishment that makes the operator look pretty or important. There are many of this nature and, in magic, they have no place.

The magician enters the place of work having made sure that, throughout the operation, there will be no external disturbances. Doors will be locked, phones turned off or unplugged, etc.

The magician may well go through another structured process of personal preparation, for in this situation, too much is better than too little.

The temple is then constructed with focussed deliberation. It does not matter which tried and tested method is used, only that it is done properly, and if it is done properly, there will be a sense of awe that can be experienced but never described.

This is the moment when the work is envisaged, ensouled and released.

Once the work is done, the magician will, with proper respect to the highest, close the temple and all that was used will be carefully put away in its rightful place.

Finally, by a deliberate act of will, the magician is earthed using whatever technique is known to be successful.

It is interesting to observe that, the more experienced and able practitioners of magic become, the less likely they are to use magic for dealing with the mundane problems of the manifest world. For, as the practitioners' understanding, vision and experience grow, they question more and more the reasons for using their skills. Their way of serving changes with this expansion of consciousness and their priorities often differ from those around them. Each one finds their own way and follows their chosen path.

It will also be observed that once this inner conviction is established, they will not resort to compromise just to please those who are near. Nor will a reason necessarily be given for their actions, mostly because it is beyond an easy explanation.

They will serve and give in their own chosen way.

16

A UNIVERSAL SYMBOL

Earth

Is this all one and is it all?
Is it lost and of the fall?
Some will say that it is.
But none really know.

Some describe it as a place of darkness and some as a place to rest the feet. Some say it is a place of new beginnings and some a place of dread and foreboding. Some see it as all that exists and some as clinging mud. None can say that they really know although there are those that do. What light is here filters through from the intermittent sightings of the sun. There is moisture here that nourishes and there is air borrowed from above. Here is life that is sustained by the journey of the sun. Not dead, not inert, but earth of earth; the finest earth striving for perfection.

I spread my roots through its channels, caverns and crevices, through soil, through sod and through earthly souls. In the way of my kind it is an anchor. In the way of my kind it has a purpose and a part of me is found in every manifest thing.

Water

Is this the great receiver?
Is this the great deceiver?
Some will say that it is.
But none really know.

It is hard to rise. It is a difficult journey, striving, rising, growing inch by inch through the place where there is nothing to cling to but fluidity. Sometimes it is calm, but mostly it is in turmoil, a turmoil caused by every single thing that lives therein: the growing things, the moving things, the rising things, the falling things, the thoughtful things and the lost. All are living things. They are in flood. They blind the senses with their endless changes, forming and evaporating only to form again in another way. Sometimes they are wise but mostly they are not. Affected from below by activity and rhapsody. Affected from below by a cacophony and chaos. Affected from above by that which a hand can cling to and trust.

My nature is thus. I am unaffected. I span all ways and I am in all places. Know that I can find a way in this chaotic fluidity. I can find a way for dreams hold no fear for me. I know them for what they are meant to be. I have spread myself through the turbulence. I have spread myself upon the turbulence. Only I am free. I have spread myself as one who knows the bitter, bitter sea. I have spread myself as one who knows the secret primal sea.

Air

> *Is this the step to evolution?*
> *Is this the upward revolution?*
> *Some will say that it is.*
> *But none really know.*

A light, a sound. I open my eye. I look to my home in the glorious sky and contemplate the unsung song.

Sounds from below rasp and grate, sounds from below annoy and vexate. Except, of course, the rare ones that resonate with the ones that emanate from the sky, from on high. These rare sounds fall on me and I take them into the water. There the call goes out in ever widening circles and a few will hear. And the ones who hear take them into the earth. They then reply. They use the echo to return the blessing and it is enough. It thrills through my being and opens my eye, open to my home in the glorious sky. Their word is revealed in my seeing.

There are some who strive to learn of thoughts that are universally secret. Many thoughts ride upon the waters. Most of them are smashed and scattered by its turbulence. Some thoughts, however, work in another way. They are controlled thoughts; they have power within. They are driven by a need to know the sky again. These "thoughts of power" are neither good nor bad, for that concept does not exist in the light of the sky. It is a concept of the earth. The only measure is what is right, and what is right is a blessing. If these "thoughts of power" are right, I will let them in and through me. They will find their way above, and they will find their way below. A union greatly sought.

The "thoughts of power" that purify are the "thoughts of power" that open my eye. I flourish in their rightness and reflect in perfect whiteness the light in the sky above, the eye in the sky above, the glory of the sun.

Fire

Is this the last communion?
Is this the place of union?
Some will say that it is.
But none really know.

Those who come to know my worth will know that I consist of many parts. A part of me is beyond time. I am as alive now as I was in ancient Egypt, or as I was in dynastic China, or as I was in Tibet of old. I am always one and the same. Nor do I suffer the restrictions of place for a part of me is universal. I am found in the west and in the exotic east, I am found in city states and biblical feasts, I am found on quiet paths and in market squares, I am among the stars and I am even in that unknown place where lies the eternity that none can understand. I am a bridge that cannot be seen, I am a vehicle that transports souls to any place, or any dimension, or any state of being. Even unto the original light.

Above and below

Is this a place beyond resistance?
Is this the place of all existence?
Some will say that it is.
But none really know.

Some know me as the water lily, others as the lotus. Some only know my flower. They know nothing of my journey through the waters or of my transferring power.

If you see me in vision, know that I am not a thing. I have no form and the beauty of my image is but fleeting. I live. I live in all that there is: from the mud to the fire, from the trees to the sea, from woman to man, yea, in eternity. I live. For if I did not, how could my symbol be so universal?

> *I do not tire.*
> *I do not sleep.*
> *I need no rest.*
> *I cannot weep,*
> *For I breathe eternal breath.*
> *My vigil spans all ages*
> *And my soul encompasses*
> *The souls of every living thing.*
> *For I breathe eternal breath.*

I am one among many. Most only refer to my bloom, forgetting the depth and the height, forgetting the east and the south, the west and the north, forgetting my roots in the soul, forgetting the need to be whole.

17

THE BOOK OF BOOKS

We live in a time when there are more published books on magic and mysticism than there have ever been. Books, books and more books. The mix is just the same as it ever was. There are a few very good books followed by a lot of books restating the words of the good books in a personal way; the motive of the writers ranging from an egotistical desire to be a teacher to a simple statement of the author's personal progression. Then there are hosts of books that are of little or no use whatsoever to any serious student. These latter books offer to take the mystery out of the mysteries, they claim to be idiots guides to illumination and knowledge, they claim to cure all ills and troubles, to show people how to have great power and other such wishful thinking. The shelves are full of them.

If asked, can a student of the occult learn from books alone? The answer would have to be, "No, unless he or she is a particularly exceptional person". It can be done, but it is achieved very rarely. However, let us not totally discourage the serious seeker.

Before practicing the inner way, it is necessary to have a genuine experience of esoteric magic. Such an experience is more than a warm glow, or a rush of emotion, or a flash of light, or a sense of presence, or an awareness of charged energy. All of these may be involved, but they alone are not an experience of the inner way, nor can such an experience be described.

Except for the rarest of people, the only way to gain this experience is by having the guidance of a genuine practitioner, a practitioner who also has the ability to pass on the way to others. Sadly, they too are rare, but it is possible to find them, for, when the pupil is ready, the teacher will appear. The seeker should not give up.

As previously stated, it would be wrong to totally discourage the serious student. Benefit can be gained from reading, but not in the way that most people would expect. There are books that offer whole systems of magic, but the real ones of these demand of the reader years of practice and discipline without external guidance. For example, Franz Bardon wrote such a book. If anyone is able to master these ways, who are we to discourage them. But you are seriously advised to be very wary of books that offer whole systems in a short period of time.

Let us move on to other writings. A genuine book will not "spell it out". Instead, contained within the pages will be words that stimulate the reader in a way that the reader does not fully understand. There is a feeling of something more that has to be pursued. The same book will offer a little practical information, but no more, just enough to point the reader in a certain direction. It is both frustrating and awesome at the same time, for the reader knows that this will be a worthwhile pursuit, but that it will not be easy. Such books will appear in various guises spanning from academic weighty tomes to excellent works of fiction. Those involved in the esoteric world will, of course, recognise this to be the way of all true practitioners, for it is a journey, a process and a living thing. Those who have "found the answer" have only found a locked door.

There is a book, the book of books
Hidden from the eye.
There is a book, the book of books
Beyond both truth and lie.

Here are some of the pitfalls that will be encountered when learning from books. Every reader will latch on to the bits they know, or are at home with, or find easy. Because of this, they will exclude the parts of the book that they do not understand. By excluding, or avoiding, or glossing over the difficult parts they effectively fail to gain the experience that they seek. Only half a system is not a system at all. A guide would insist on the pupil learning everything and help by giving clues to the way through those difficult parts. We can only learn what we do not know, and we cannot learn that unless there is a guiding hand to push us back to the parts we avoided.

Another common error is to only look for the pretty or the light and exclude all aspects that are unpleasant and uncomfortable. A whole system is a whole system. Nothing in life or magic can be without the shadow.

Another pitfall is snacking. That is, picking what are perceived to be the best bits from different sources. It is a remarkably common practice and it fails to work for the same reason that avoiding the difficult bits fails. It is, in fact, a more extreme version of the same error.

When writing about books, it would be right to include a few words on holy books. Holy books belong to both the great religions of the world and to the smallest of religious communities. Each will have their own book and will use it for guidance.

Holy books tend to be read in the exoteric way by the vast majority of members of these religious communities. In the extreme, all the words are taken literally and no allowance for interpretation is tolerated. This usually applies only to a few exoteric followers. Most people in these communities will interpret the words in the light of the earthly world as it pertains to them at that particular time.

For the few who are esoteric followers of a religion, they will read their holy book in another way. They will recognise that it can be read on many levels. They will recognise the symbolism within the words. They will know that the words, properly understood, can become keys to another way of knowing. They will study their book using contemplative and meditative techniques, stretching their abilities so that the words can be studied using all of their faculties, not just the intellect and the restrictive rational thought processes that deny the existence of those things that are considered to be illogical.

Let no one be under the illusion, however, that this is the way of the dreamer. It is not. To a properly trained person it is vital to work within a strong discipline thereby enabling that person to distinguish between fantasy and the reality that transcends the manifest.

It should also be mentioned that a book can be used purely as a symbol, for all the things symbolised by a book are of value. The symbol of the book, when used in magical work, is an excellent tool for those seeking a greater understanding and an enhanced ability in the pursuit of their chosen work.

Another valuable book is the book that slowly comes together over time as the students record their experiences and write down those techniques and methods that have been developed and found to work. There are also those rare and humbling gems that are given in a way that the receiver alone will understand.

I offer you words, not comfort.
I offer you trials, not ease.
I offer you that which is needed
To travel Her turbulent seas.
Use the words,
'Tis the way of priestess and priest.

The serious student knows that the precious gifts of Hermes, or Mercury, or Thoth will always be passed on to the worthy.

There is no writing in the book of books.
The pages are blank and clean.
There are no words, no symbols seen.
No place behind, betwixt, between.
Look not upon these pages
Until the eye is open.
Look not upon these pages
Until the word is spoken.
Look not upon these pages
Until the key is broken

A final statement.

Yes, the writer is aware that these words are yet another addition to the pile.

18

THE WORD LEAST UNDERSTOOD

Those versed in the way of esoteric magic will understand the strong reluctance that is felt when the need arises to write about love. Because of its very complex and emotive nature, it is a task not easily taken on. The need has arisen and here follow some words on the subject. They are, of course, inadequate, as all such words must be.

It is so often found that when new initiates begin to develop a little magical ability, they become aware of something within telling them that love is the way. This influence will cause many among them to go down the path of an earthly concept of love. For some there is a blind acceptance and naivety that is outwardly harmless and becomes an end in itself. Others will leave the way of esoteric magic and enter into a world of mysticism. Some will find a practical way of realising their earthly vision of love. Others will become well meaning and full of good intentions, but will not be taken seriously. Others will dwell in an illusory world of the good and beautiful. A few special people will follow a path of self-sacrifice and devotion to a chosen cause that will be an example to us all. Virtually all of these will leave the inner way behind them for as long as it takes them to work through their newfound ideals.

The ones who stay with the way of magic will be, in the main, the ones who questioned the meaning of the word love, and the search of lifetimes begins.

The questions are many. Let us start with the more obvious. For example, when the lioness kills to feed her young, is she wrong? Does the killing invalidate her love for her young? Is love the right word to use for her desire to ensure that they are fed and kept safe from harm? Can these questions be answered by human intellectual processes? Is putting a crawling thing out into the frost on a winters night more loving than killing it instantly or, better still, letting it share your room? Is doting upon the needs of those around a loving act or are these people being denied the means to live their own lives because the benevolence of the giver is always at hand? Will the polar bear stop hunting its prey because the victim wants to give it a hug? Will love stop the invading army? Should we say, "Welcome mighty warrior, here is my home, share it"? Should our love be for our fellow humans or for everything? If we decide that it is for everything, how can we live except by killing those we love, be they animals, plants or the good bacteria in a loaf of bread?

Every action has a reaction, so how true is the phrase, "The road to hell is paved with good intentions".

Pages could be written along these lines, endless words about moral and emotional dilemmas.

If love has a meaning in the way of all things it is not going to be found by pursuing these types of earthly-based arguments. They are effects, not causes. We need to look to that which is behind all. We must remember that the word was given to some of those who chose the inner way. Therefore it is towards the inner way that they must look for an understanding or, more accurately, a path towards an understanding.

Initiates of the western mystery tradition will learn of forces that influence manifestation. They are known in many forms, elemental, sephirothic, planetary, god and goddess forces and so on. In this paper we will consider them as planetary forces.

Let us start with Jupiter. In Jupiter we have benevolent aspects such as mercy, good order, beneficence, stability and so on. All are very worthy aspects of nature and, in mortal terms, they can be simplistically thought of as loving. But that would be to deny the more extreme aspects of Jupiterian force such as tyranny and oppressive control personified in the more ruthless regimes of particular monarchs.

In Mars we have courage and strength, but we also have cruelty and destruction that can be wielded without any sign of reason or thought. Once set in motion, this aspect of Martian power is incredibly difficult to control. How can this be resolved in love?

In Venus there is a power that affects humans in a host of ways. Powerful emotions are stirred through the arts, through sexual desire and through raw instinct. The love that people identify with Venus is a fickle thing indeed. It is far too volatile to answer the questions being asked by the initiate.

In Mercury we have the prospect of wisdom; we have the ability to soar to all places in a wonderful quest for knowledge. Harnessing Mercurial force enables the practitioner of magic to influence through the use of knowledge and control. But as with all of these forces, how they are used is entirely the choice of the practitioner. The forces are the forces; they have no bias. The answer does not seem to lie here.

In the Moon we have a world of dreams, visions, illusion, astral effluent, phantasms, etc. Every form can be found in this force that lies just behind the manifest. It can be used, or more accurately, it must be mastered, by those practicing the inner way. But it hardly seems a haven for transcendental love. The best it can offer is an illusion or impression of love.

In Saturn we have a force that tests all to the limits. The love that is in this test will most certainly not conform to that conceived by people in the manifest world, for its outward form is stern indeed.

In the Sun we have a hint of love that can be defined. The unselfish love of sacrifice, the love of all sacrificed gods and saints. It is the mystery of the crucifixion. In the Sun we also have a harmony and devotion that is unworldly. It is a force that is life, but also a force that holds the mystery of death. Sadly, there is also a dark side to the Sun. This dark side is shown in humans as pomposity, pride and overbearing righteousness. Even the Sun force must have an opposite, a control, to reflect and balance its glory. The Sun alone is not a place to seek the answer, but in the Sun we may have a clue to where our quest should be directed and that is the influence beyond and behind these planetary forces of nature.

As all of these forces have dual aspects, so is this duality universal to all that exists with but one exception.

Let us contemplate original duality so often described in legends and scriptures, the legends of goddesses and gods. Let us then realise that all gods are one god and all goddesses are one goddess. They are the universal Father and the universal Mother, the pillars of the universe and of every temple. Duality is universal. There is black and there is white. There is life and there is death. There is that which is manifest and there is that which is not. The list can go on forever.

Duality is founded in the original division out of that which is beyond knowing. When the original division took place, two attractions were created. They are beautifully expressed in Crowley's Book of the Law,

"...*Divided for love's sake, for the chance of union*".

The first attraction is the attraction between the two parts that are divided. The second attraction follows this union of millions of years, for it is the attraction to the One from whence all came.

This explanation seems simple. It is not. It is but one symbolic representation.

> Be cleansed in beauty.
> Be cleansed by fire.
> Be cleansed by mercy.
> Call into the dark, the vast, the endless space.
> See sorrow, know hollow, be truly alone.
> Die in that place again and again,
> But not in illusion.
> Know, not assume.
> Know, not pretend.
> Go there and know
> The ultimate end that can never end.
> She will be waiting.
> Unknown, unknowable,
> All.

The writer of these words has as little understanding of the mystery of universal love as has any other involved in the quest. The ideal has been put before us all and each will work towards and within that ideal in their own way. These words are but a stimulant that may help direct the searcher to that which is ever beyond.

19

A SPARK OF WONDER

It could be called a wakening, the parallels are strong.
It could be called enlightening, but that would be quite wrong.
Oh yes she was aware, aware as never before,
Aware of her total ignorance on a new and troubled shore.

She had seen the spark of wonder.

She planned to use her days away from things that must be done.
From work, from home, from shallow fun, to climb the rocks, to journey on.
To sacred places she would go and call from deep within,
"I'll journey through this land I've seen, but how do I begin?"

A real call is always answered, but the one who asks does not always listen to the answer.

How many days would pass her by, how many days to yearn?
How many times did she utter her cry? How many ways to learn?
The darkness is a real thing; the darkness holds the key,
The darkness is unknown to her, but a guide has heard her plea.

The dark one watches and waits.

Words are put her way and images bright and clear.
She meets someone, a guiding one, a temporary seer.
She finds that words have meaning and the symbols start to live.
A good first step, but not enough, for she must learn to give.

A simple secret of the inner way.

The dark one is a relentless one, for time is in his hands.
The dark one alone can open the door to her new found hidden lands.
The dark one is an unseen guide, stern and from the night.
As it is written, the teacher will come when the pupil is ready and right.

She becomes a witch.

Not a witch of fairyland, not a witch on show,
But one who follows the inner way, a way that they won't know.
A witch who knows the seasons, as tides beyond the earth;
As part of the greater reason, of life and death and birth.

Symbols and forces and the way of evolution.

She took a name, a secret name and lived within its core.
For a witches name is a potent thing, an opening, a door;
And once the step is taken to the place that lies beyond
A new name must be chosen, a new and living bond.

Living the life.

Not by inch, nor ounce, nor hour but by another gauge,
She learned to give in the way that is right, the knowing of a sage.
She stood before the mountain path vanishing above
And she aspired to climb those steps and learn the way of love.

Naked before the highest.

Vows before the Goddess, vows before the God,

Vows before the Infinite One, her spine became Their rod.
Initiations. Verity, not titles brash and grand.
For true initiations take humility in hand.

Are you willing to suffer to learn?

Magic is a simple thing, in principle at least,
But learning to work with the forces beyond is to master the wildest beast.
Properly prepared, trained and able is the only way
To let in the light from the darkness of night and bless the newfound day.

A spark of wonder.

Magic is a technical thing, but not a limitation.
The ways are known, ritual, throne, trance, meditation,
Temple sleep, mantra and weep for hours in dedication.
Concentrate, control, relate, but never a limitation.

And each way must be followed in its wholeness.

She used the words, the wildest words, the words that tear asunder.
An Echo of the word of words, sending out its wonder.
These words are more than earthly words, they open up the veil.
Control these words and they become a rudder, oar and sail.

Make it happen.

She stood before the altar of the Mighty Three.
Goddess, God and Infinite One, The Crown, Eternity.
The flame within would not relent, initiate was she,
For once that death has taken place there is no liberty.

But always she is free.

Care, care and yet more care in everything she did.
There is no other way and yet, the wise will not forbid,
Free will is ours and we must choose the method and the way.
But those who prize the words of the wise will not go astray.

Properly prepared we must always be.

She practiced the wholeness of her craft as a witch of the inner way
In a temple built between the worlds within the purist ray.
With roots on the earth and roots in the void in the living of her quest
The current flowed 'twixt above and below and her work was lovingly blessed.

Only by giving can a work be done.

Texts she read many and long, most in the form of a book.
But thankful was she for the guiding hand of the one who held the crook.
For a book alone is a troublesome thing, it gives and it deceives,
For how can we know the important parts that are hidden in its leaves?

A warning.

Though old and wise in the way of the craft, a student she will remain,
Learning more and knowing less as they ask her to explain.

"It is yours to find, not mine", she says, "I can but show a way".

And with the word least understood,
The one that is given the name of love,
She'll pass away.

For she is a loving lady.

THE CLOSING

There isn't a closing.